How To Save Money For Entrepreneurs

30 Strategies To Grow Your Bank Account and Enjoy Life Debt Free

Argena Olivis

www.ArgenaOlivis.com

Bonus: Download Your Free Kindle Book Creation Course

Learn how to create and market your first kindle book online.

You can use this course to get started making money online.

Plus, when you subscribe you'll receive my best tips and tutorials for online business success.

Learn how I'm making money from the following methods: kindle publishing, affiliate marketing, email marketing, information products, blogging, and more.

Visit www.argenaolivis.com/freekindlecourse2/ for access

Table of Contents

Introduction

You NEED to save money. As a business owner it's most likely that you have an inner desire for wealth creation, investing, and growing your income. So why aren't you saving money? It's because you lack the right strategies or mindset to get started.

Saving money is important, obviously. But sometimes we need to be reminded of the reasons why. What are some of the reasons that people like you and I need to save money?

I can think of a good one: When you're self-employed or a business owner, you never know what may go down. Although, we may control a small portion of our income, sometimes we have better months than others.

Unless your business will forever increase its revenue, you need savings in order to give yourself a sense of security (way better than job security), and have money stocked away **just in case things get real.**

You're also able to **protect your family**; imagine having enough money saved in case of emergencies, to send your children to college, to create memories by vacationing, and to help someone who is struggling financially. That would feel pretty damn good, at least that would give me motivation outside of saving for myself.

And here's the biggie: When you become a saver, you put yourself in a situation for more opportunities. While everyone else around you is broke, you're able to put your wallet where you mouth is and **take part of any opportunity of your choice, immediately.**

Why I Wrote This Book

My name is Argena Olivis, and I wrote this book because I'm passionate about teaching and connecting with like-minded entrepreneurs such as yourself.

I didn't used to be a saver. I mean... I was never a crazy spender, but I was having a hard time saving money. My husband and I would try to put money aside for things, and it seems like something always came up that would wipe out our savings and we would be back living paycheck to paycheck.

Then I attended the Millionaire Mind Intensive Seminar a while back and it really engrained in me how important it is to manage your money.

I took action on what I learned, and I was able to save over $2,000 within 6 months, and I have no debt but student loans. They may not sound like a lot to you, but for my income and lifestyle at the time; that's was a decent amount to save within such a short period of time.

Before you even read this book... I hope you're willing to be independent in this. This is something I did for myself. That means, I have my own separate savings account. Although my husband and I share another joint savings account, I found that holding myself accountable and really putting my mind to this is what put me ahead.

Unfortunately, sometimes you have to do things for yourself to really get the ball rolling; if a spouse is not ready to make that change, it just is what it is. They will come around when they're ready, it doesn't mean they're bad people, it just means that they have different habits from you and you don't want to put that strain on the relationship.

It's not worth it. By the way, no, this is not a relationship book... but I think it's an extremely important part of saving and may be why so many entrepreneurs are held back.

Keep in mind that at the end of the day, it's not even about the amount, **it's about building the habit.** Habits are what makes us successful. We'll get into developing money management habits later in this book.

Since I had so much success with the strategies I used, I wanted to share them with you. Because I know you can benefit from this information. **I know you need this information.**

How To Read This Book

I want you to take action on every single chapter so you can master the information in this book. The best way to read this book is by **reading one chapter**, putting that information into action and getting results with it, and then moving on to the next.

Or... You may want to read the entire book thoroughly and then go back to chapter 1 and begin taking action if you're too curious about what information is contained in this book (I don't blame you.) But the most important thing here is you taking action and start developing money saving habits.

There will be action steps at the end of each chapter so you know EXACTLY what you should be doing.

Oh, and remember to have fun. Saving money is super fun and it **helps you to build confidence**. Once you start saving and you see all those zeros in your bank account, you'll feel amazing.

I'd love to hear about your progress and testimonials. You can contact me at any time by emailing me.

Chapter 1: Mindset Shift

"Don't limit yourself. Many people limit themselves to what they think they can do. You can go as far as your mind lets you. What you believe, remember, you can achieve. ~Mary Kay Ash

Just like any success in life, you're going to need to believe in yourself and have to right mindset in order to achieve your goals. Many people just look for the strategies and never take action on them. They get addicted to learning new tips and tricks, but they still don't have any results.

This is because they don't take action, and they don't take action because they don't believe in themselves or don't have the motivation and discipline rise above their doubts. So, the first thing you need to do is believe that this process will work.

Once you believe in the process, you will be consistent in your savings and eliminating debt, and you'll be able to hit your savings goals and milestones.

How to become a saver and not a spender

I now want you to consider yourself a saver, once you label yourself as that, your actions are likely to follow. Tell yourself every day that you're a saver, write it down where you can see it, and start taking the actions to become one.

There will be hurdles and distractions, it's inevitable. People will test your faith in the process and try to invite you out shopping, get you to spend money on things you don't need, and things will come up where you feel you want to spend money unnecessarily.

This happens when you have a new goal, people test you, and the universe tests you. If you can get through those hurdles and have a strong belief and reasons for saving for what you want. You will be a successful saver.

Saving is a habit to be proud of, because many people don't save

and are one check away from being broke.

How to develop money saving habits

Like any habit that you want to create, it starts with action. So your

first task would be to open a savings account and begin putting

money away **every time you get paid.**

As soon as you get any form of money, no matter if it's from a

birthday card or from a sale you made, when the money hits your

bank account immediately transfer 10% of it from your checking

account to your savings account.

It doesn't matter the amount. I don't care if you made only a $3

sale, transfer the money. If you don't know how to figure 10% out,

you can simply multiply the amount of money you made by 0.10.

Or you can download a percentage calculator app on your phone.

You can do more than 10%, but I don't recommend you doing less.

Next, don't touch your savings for any reason. If an emergency comes up, try to make some extra money or find another way to get it, but **don't touch your savings account for at least six months**.

So now you have two simple habits to work on creating: saving 10% of everything you make, and not touching your savings account.

If you can master these two habits, you're well on your way. Try it for 30 days, and see how you bank account increases along with your confidence.

Think long term

"The ability to discipline yourself to delay gratification in the short term in order to enjoy greater rewards in the long term, is the indispensable prerequisite to success." – Brian Tracy

The most successful entrepreneurs of all time think long term. Thinking long term helps to make a shift in your brain that gives you the muscle and discipline to sacrifice and turn down short term pleasure for long term results.

So anytime you're faced with a challenge and want to spend money, think long and hard if it's a good investment long term. Will spending the money benefit you in the long run? If you base your decisions off long term thinking, you will be able to do what others aren't able to in the future.

Think about how saving today will set you and your family up for a better tomorrow. Be willing to **give up instant gratification** and think about how your future will be once you are focused on increasing your income and your savings.

You can live your ideal life, you just have to be willing to put in the work. There is no such thing as an overnight success. Keep your head down and keep grinding to the point where you are doing so well financially, that money will never be a worry for you again.

Be confident in not spending money, but investing in yourself

As you save money, your confidence will grow. Overtime, if you develop the correct habit, touching your savings won't even cross your mind. I remember my third month or so into saving, I had an emergency come up with my car and I had to pay to get it fixed. I had to find money in other places, I didn't even think about touching my savings, in fact, I forgot I even had a savings in that situation.

We make things work when we develop the right habits. Make a vowel to yourself that you are dedicated to this process and don't let anyone or any circumstance set you back.

If you're thinking about touching your money, think about how you would get the money if you didn't have a savings. Because obviously, you've found ways before if you're reading this book.

Just remember: Touching Your Money Is NOT an Option

Sacrifice: what are you willing to give up

It's not that easy. You're going to have to give up something if you want to have something new. You will have to sacrifice, not forever, but long enough until you hit your goals.

This may mean less entertainment, and more work. The great thing about this is, once you create more income, you can eventually add more entertainment back in your life such as travel, going out to eat, etc. But for now, you have a new goal that you MUST achieve.

Depending on what your income is and what your savings goal is for the year, you may be able to save while still doing a lot of the things you love.

For Example: If you have a high income, you may just need to develop better money saving habits instead of spending every penny you make. But, if you have a low income, you may want to cut down on the fun until you increase your income and hit your savings goals.

You will also need to develop the habit of budgeting. If you're spending more than you make—there's a problem. We will be learning about budgeting in chapter 4.

Action Steps:

1. Believe that you are a saver, repeat this to yourself daily and write it down somewhere you'll see it everyday

2. Open a savings account

3. Every time you get paid, transfer 10% into that bank account (habit)

4. Do NOT touch your savings for any reason (habit)

Chapter 2: Create a Financial Freedom Plan

"By failing to prepare, you're preparing to fail" –Benjamin Franklin

You don't know where you're going unless you have a road map. In this chapter we're going to come up with a plan for your savings goals. Use this plan daily so you'll continue to go in the right direction.

Money Saving Goals

The first thing you want to do is list no more than three items or events you want to save for. The reason you don't want more than three at a time is because you don't want to get overwhelmed. There are many things you may want to save up for: vacation, contingency fund, a new business venture, a house, a car, etc.

Next, you want to determine how much you want to save per month or by the end of the year. So for example, you may want to have $3,000 in your contingency fund by the end of the year; or you want to save $250 a month towards your contingency fund.

There are benefits to saving for the year and the month.

With the monthly savings goal, you'll have consistency and know exactly how much is going in each month, and how much you'll have at the end of the year. The only problem with that is you may not have enough income coming in right now to support that number. So if your income increases, you're saving less.

The great thing about the yearly goal is, you save what you can at the income level your currently at. This system encourages you to increase your income so you can hit your goal before the year ends.

Keep in mind that the time frames are up to you. If you want to go on vacation in six months because you plan on working hard on your business, you may want to save $800 in six months.

So, no matter what your money saving goals are, make sure you're **specific in the amount and the time frame.** The "how to" will be dependent on your mindset and the actions you take.

<u>**Exercise:**</u> Take out your journal or notebook and write down your money saving goals. *For example*: my money saving goals for next year is to save $10,000 in my contingency fund, $5,000 towards a house, and $2,000 for vacations.

Contingency Fund

We've talked a little about contingency funds, but you may be wondering exactly what it is. A contingency fund is basically an "emergency fund". This is a savings that you should NEVER touch unless you truly need to.

The word "contingency" is much better than "emergency" because if you save for an emergency, you're bound to have one. So I don't like to put that negative energy into the universe by using the word "emergency" when it comes to my hard earned money.

In this fund, you'll be saving up for your living expenses. So depending on how much you make a month, you want to save between 3 months-1 years' worth of money.

For example: If you live of $2,000 a month. You want to have $6,000 or more put away at any given time.

Once you save your desired amount for your contingency fund, you will **increase your confidence in business and your life.** It will eliminate lot of fear, and set you apart from the average American who has either no money saved or would only be able to survive 3 months or less if they lost their current income.

Believe me, you don't want to be a statistic that lives paycheck to paycheck. Give yourself and your family a peace of mind by putting money aside in your contingency fund today.

How will you increase your business income?

Now that you see the value in a contingency fund, and you know your other savings goals. You now need to decide how you will increase your business income.

I love writing this book for entrepreneurs, because the average person can't increase their income, because they have a cap. It's a sad reality, but true. But you on the other hand, have unlimited potential as an entrepreneur.

Bring out that pen and paper again and write down some ideas on how you can increase your income over the next year.

Here are some ideas: create more products, add more services, increase subscribers, get better sales conversions, etc.

What can you add, test, or tweak that you know will increase your income. For now on, focus on income producing activities first when creating your to-do list.

Stay organized

Stay organized in your business, this will reduce overwhelm and increase your income. Make sure to pay close attention to things that matter. Work in an area that inspires you, without a lot of clutter.

Keep a separate bank account for our taxes. Ask your CPA what percentage you should be saving for each payment you get.

For example: For every book sale you may have to put away 20%.

Make sure you know your numbers so you don't have to run around when it's tax season trying to figure out how much you made, or how much you owe.

Even if you have a lot of business expenses, still put aside that amount because you never know. Even if you do end of being refunded, at least you'll have that money set aside "just in case".

Make it a habit to determine your income for the month "after taxes".

Keep good records, or have someone keep good records for you. Get tax software and make sure you're looking at how much you spent and how much you made each month. Don't wait until the last minute to get these things together.

What can you get rid of?

This is the scary part, think about what you can get rid of, at least until you're making more money. What things do you have that you don't really use, or are willing to sacrifice in order to save more money?

Things like subscriptions you don't use. Can you giving out eating out? Maybe you can eat out once a week. Or your car note? Maybe instead, you can pay for your car in cash.

Start thinking about what you can get rid of that can bring in more income that you can put towards your savings goals.

Action steps:

1. post your money saving goals

2. open your contingency fund

3. get tax software and keep up to date with how much your spending

4. get rid of __(insert money suck here)___

Chapter 3: 30 Strategies to Create and Automate Money Saving Habits

"Successful people are simply those with successful habits." ~Brian Tracy

1. Use Auto Transfer

If you have a problem with developing a habit to transfer money to your savings account as soon as you get paid, consider setting up an automatic transfer. You can easily do this by going into your bank, or, you may be able to set it up online yourself.

Deeply consider this option for it makes life easier. Even if it's not the full amount you want to save, it's still a handy tool that will save you time and mental space that you can use to think about other important things in your life and business.

2.   Set Aside 10%

As soon as you get any money, automatically set aside ten percent. This is an easy rule to remember and implement. Start with the habit when you get your very next sale or payment.

This applies to any money that comes in. It doesn't matter rather it's an anniversary card or a dollar you found on the street, set aside 10% and watch your savings grow!

3.   Go On A Money Saving Challenge

Make things fun and challenge yourself. Make it a goal to not spend any money except for on necessities for 30 days. These types of challenges will help you develop confidence in your savings. It will also help you develop a discipline for not spending money.

When you do this challenge, you will see how well you can survive with the basics. It gives you an appreciation for what you have.

4. Get Inspired

Start looking at magazines, images, social media, and television for things that you want to save for. On top of your contingency fund, you can also save for other things that will bring you pleasure and reward you for your hard work.

Rather it's a new car, a home, or a vacation to Jamaica; make it your business to save for things that will be an investment in your joy.

5. No Car Note

I was happy that I started reading books and watching videos about managing my money long ago. This helped me to avoid having a car note. The way I bought my car was I saved up for it and purchased it (used of course).

If you can, do the same. If you're already in contract, think about if your car is something that is holding you back from financial freedom. If you can comfortably fit the car payment into your budget, then let it be.

The scary thing about a car note is if you stop paying it you're automatically out of luck because you don't own it. Plus, they charge you so much interest on the loan it makes me sick.

If you have to have a car note, I understand. But if you can, avoid it like the plague!

6. Stop Eating Out

Cook at home, and have fun doing it. If you don't know how to cook, go on YouTube and follow the instructions on how to make your meals. It kills me when I used to see people whom I worked with running their money over to eat out every day for lunch and buying snacks for the vending machines.

I had a completely different mindset, because I was wishing I was the one owning the vending machines!

Eating out can be healthier, it saves you tons of money, and cooking can be a relaxing thing. Either cut down the amount of eating out you do in a week, or cut it out completely except for special occasions.

Me? I usually eat out once or twice a week. Once with my husband on date night, and then sometimes I don't feel like cooking (guilty as charged!)

7. **Couponing**

No, I'm not some die-hard couponing queen because **I don't have time**. I'd rather spend my time creating more products to sell so I can make more money. But coupons do come in handy at times. But if you're interested in being a die-hard coupon person, more power to you, because it's a full time job within itself!

I usually don't use coupons for food, because the coupons for food are usually super unhealthy or so expensive I wouldn't buy it anyway. But every time I get the coupon fliers in the mail I skim through them to see if they have any coupons for things I know I'll actually buy, like: soup, toothpaste, hair care products, etc.

I immediately clip these coupons because I know I'm going to use them and then toss the rest of the fliers. I don't care what sales or going on at what stores because I shop at a one location and by time you drive to all these stores to get these sales, you're wasting your time and gas.

So I do use coupons, but only for the things I know I'm going to buy. Make sure to keep the coupons in your wallet or purse, you don't want to forget them when it's time to go shopping. Yes, this does help me save a few hundred bucks a year instead of paying full price for these items.

8. Make It A Habit To Be Early

It pays to be early sometimes, you can save a lot of money by doing so. By knowing your schedule and planning ahead, you can save big bucks on things like travel, events, tickets, and more. The early bird gets the worm.

That's why it's important to have goals in business and life. And once you save money, you can jump on opportunities immediately and not have to wait to save up for them.

9. Book Trips and Hotels Using Travel Sites

I don't play around when it comes to this. I use Hotwire and Expedia to book my hotels and flights. They are both legit and it saves me hundreds of dollars a year. You'll be surprised how cheap of hotels you can find on Hotwire (make sure they're 4 or 5 start hotels).

I save hundreds of dollars by booking flights with Expedia rather than going directly to the airline's websites. It just makes more sense. Also, make sure to book your flights as early as possible, usually the earlier the cheaper, and you get a better choice of seats.

10. Cheap Alternatives For Entertainment

You don't have to spend a ton of money to be entertained. I don't even have cable, if I want to watch something I have Netflix, and Hulu. And if I'm feeling really fancy, I might rent a DVD from the Redbox. But there's also free options, check your local library, they have DVDs and CD's!

If you're looking for entertainment, research things that you can do that cost little to no money.

You don't have to spend money going to a fancy dinner, you can have a candlelight dinner at home or walk around the park.

Invite friends over to party instead of going out or before going out. Buy your own bottle instead of paying bar prices, I hate buying overpriced drinks at restaurants and bars. But I know money won't be an object soon when I become a multimillionaire.

But until you have more than enough money to blow, keep saving and increasing your income so you can live the lavish lifestyle you work so hard towards. You want to be smart with your money, wouldn't you rather invest in a new business than buy $80 worth of drinks at the bar tonight?

11. Buy Used or Borrow from the Library

Your car may not be the only thing you want to buy used. Things that cost tons of money like big appliances, furniture, or even redecorating can be done with used items that work or look just as good.

Go to your local Goodwill or thrift store to see if you can find used items that you need. You'll be surprised, some of their items are new in the box.

12. Exercise At Home

Cancel your gym membership and exercise at home. You can simply watch YouTube videos and get a full work out. The thing is, I do look at a gym membership as an investment in your health, but if you don't use it get rid of it.

People lose weight or stay healthy by working out at home. Don't be fooled. You can save a ton of money by simply jogging outside, doing weight training in your attic, or sit ups on your yoga mat.

13. Track What You Spend

We'll go more into tracking and budgeting in chapter 4, because you do need to be aware of what you're spending. The more you track, the more adjustments you can make.

You should know exactly where your money is going each month, that way you can see where you're spending foolishly and get rid of the things you don't need or can live without for the moment while you increase your income.

14. Make Your Coffee at Home

Unless you're going to the coffee shop to work on your business, make your coffee at home. It's just so much cheaper. Those coffee drinks are overpriced and it's crazy how much money you can save by making it yourself.

15. Stick To Your Grocery Shopping List & Only Shop For The Week

Make a list before you even get to the store. Vow to yourself to stick to that list **no matter what.** Don't keep running to the grocery store, pick a day of the week to go and then go only on that day.

Only buy enough food for the week, there's no need for you to keep buying food when you haven't even ate the food in your house. If you keep buying more food than you can eat, it'll eventually go bad and you just wasted money!

How about this... don't go grocery shopping until you've eaten all the food in your house.

16. Plan For Holidays and Gift Giving In Advance

Holidays and birthdays can be a killer in your savings momentum. People I know personally have gone into debt after the holidays because of spending tons of money on expensive gifts. First off, if you don't have money like that, don't buy anyone expensive gifts.

Last year, most of my gifts I gave out were $5 or less.

Unless it's someone that's in your immediate family (children, spouse, mom, dad, etc.), there's no reason to spend a ton of money. If you plan ahead, and do the opposite of what most people do, you can save on quality gifts.

A few ways to think ahead of the crowd is to buy gifts right after the holiday season when everything is discounted, and to buy gifts when they are out of season. Like most people, don't wait until the last minute and run out to the stores when everything is overpriced. This goes back to the early bird getting the worm.

17. See If There's A Software or Automated Tool That Can Replace Employees

This is an advanced business tip. If there is software that can do the same things your employees or Virtual Assistants can do, then get the software. This will save you money in the long run. Sometimes depending on and having others work for you can leave you with a whole bunch of work to do yourself if they decide to quit or not follow through.

If you do have to have employees, Virtual Assistants, or Independent Contractors to run your business, make sure you have a system and step by step training already made up for them so they can train themselves and jump right in where the last employee left off.

You can have your current employee make these SOPs (Standard Operating Procedures) so you don't have to worry about doing it yourself, simply tell them to write up or create videos of what they do on a daily basis.

18. Be A Producer, Not A Consumer

As an entrepreneur, always be thinking like a producer. Create as much value as you can in the marketplace and be the go to person for whatever you sell. Stop consuming, especially if you want to save money.

Create more so you can sell more and save more. If you keep consuming more than you produce, then you'll go broke and continue to stay exactly where you are.

19. Plan Your Meals Ahead Of Time

This will save you tons of time and money. Plan your meals so that you can be more productive throughout the day. When you know exactly what you're going to eat, you save money by not eating out and you save time from thinking about what you're going to eat.

You can also take this as far as cooking your meals for the entire week. Simply freeze the food that you're not going to eat right away and refrigerate the rest. More productivity>more money > more savings.

20. Set Savings Goals

Having goals allows you to know exactly where you are and exactly where you want to go. It gives you a destination to work toward. If you set the right goals, you'll also get excited and motivated to follow through.

But it's not enough to set goals. You have to have reasons of why you want to achieve these goals; because reasons create results. Once you have the goals, the reasons to back them up, and the commitment; you're well on your way to financial freedom.

So start small with your goals until you develop the right habits. For example: If you do a 30 challenge, your goal can be to save $300 in 30 days.

21. Use Cash

Cash is king. Use cash because swiping a card is too easy. Studies show that when you have that physical cash in your hand, you get a little more attached when you're spending because you don't want to see it go. Opposed to a debit or credit card where you can't see that actual transaction happening.

This can also be great if you visually want to see how much you're saving. You can create a savings jar and put away money that way.

22. Choose Quality of Quantity

Cheap doesn't always mean quality. Sometimes it's worth it to spend more money if the item you buy will last longer. If you buy non-quality items, they will break easier and you'll just have to keep spending more money over time to replace them.

23. Increase Your Income

It's obvious that the more you make the more you're able to save. Increase your income by offering more products and services to your customers. Increase the price of what you sell, or create more streams of income.

If you can test and tweak and get better conversations or charge a higher price, your sales can increase drastically. That's the great thing about being a business owner, there's no cap on the amount of income you can create. So begin working on ways to increase your income, you owe it to yourself.

24. Plan Ahead

If you plan ahead, you will become unstoppable. This is because you'll know exactly what you should be doing and when, which in turn **increases productivity**. The more productive you are, the more you results you'll get.

Planning ahead is never a bad thing. *For example:* Plan out your production for the year. What projects will you be working on and when?

By planning ahead, and scheduling your success, you will increase your profits and savings exponentially.

25. Quit Bad Habits

Yeah I had to put this in here, stop the bad habits, not only are they costing you money but they're costing you your health. What's the point being a successful entrepreneur if you're not going to be around to enjoy your money?

How can you build your legacy when you're constantly smoking, drinking alcohol, and drinking soda (we call it pop here in Pittsburgh). All things are fine in moderation, but if your bad habits are costing you tons of money, maybe you should give them up until you can afford to do them.

But don't let these things cause you to go broke and ruin your health, it's totally not worth it.

26. Monitor Your Bank Account

You need to be aware. Don't be an avoider, avoiders let their bank accounts overdraft and get out of control because they're too afraid to face the disaster they created. I dare you to **look at your**

bank account daily and monitor it to make sure you're being charged what you should and looking at ways to save.

27. Do Better Accounting

Make sure you're on top of your business income and expenses. Make sure every dollar is accounted for. Take advantage of every possible tax break you can. If you haven't yet, get serious and get some tax software or hiring an accountant or data entry person to take care of this.

Once you know where you're spending, you can see where you can cut some things out or add some things in that will increase your income such as advertising and promotion.

28. Be Prepared

Make sure you're covered. Some things you just shouldn't play around with. Make sure you have your car insurance, health insurance, renters or home insurance and any other kind of insurance on lock. You don't want to be put in any situations you can't handle.

Making sure you're insured will give you a sense of confidence. Make sure to shop around for the best prices and get the best bang for your buck.

29. Use Independent Contractors

Use independent contractors or virtual assistants instead of employees. Employees cost a ton of money and sometimes it's not worth it. Of course it depends on your business. Contractors are people you can work with on an as-needed basis and you don't have to worry about other liabilities that come along with employees.

30. Become More Valuable

Last, but no least, become more valuable! By raising your value you're able to raise your prices. Learn new skills that can help you create more income streams or make you even more of an expert in your field.

Raise the value of your product by adding more to it so it can stand alone as the most valuable product of its type. By raising your value or the value of your product, you will attract more quality customers and clients and never have to fear being out of work.

Action Step:

1. Do 1 of the 30 strategies from this chapter every single day for 30 days until you've mastered them all.

Chapter 4: Budgeting

"A budget is not just a collection of numbers, but an expression of our values and aspirations." ~Jacob Lew

In this chapter, we're going to create a budget for you. I know, budget sounds like a terrible thing, but it will create more freedom in your life at the end of the day. A budget is simply a guideline that if followed can create lots of savings for you in the future.

When you stay within your budget, or go below your budget, you develop confidence within yourself to save more and make more so you can increase your spending on the things you work so hard for.

Create your Household Budget

Create your household budget by listing your monthly expenses and income. Here's an example budget for two people:

Household Monthly Income:

Job $1,500

Businesses $2,000 (after taxes)

Total Monthly Income: $3,500 a month

Monthly Expenses:

Rent/Mortgage: $500

Food: $200

Electricity: $60

Gas: $60

Car Gas: $120

Car Note: $130

Car Insurance: $113

Health Insurance: $60

Renters/Home Insurance: $15

Life Insurance: $25

Internet/Cable/Phone: $89

Loans/Credit Cards: $100

Entertainment/Pets/Clothing: $100

Total Monthly Expenses: $1,512

Total Monthly Income-**Total Monthly Exposes**= Money Left Over

From Personal Expenses

$3,500-$1,512= $1,988

Of course **these numbers will vary greatly** depending on how many people are in your household, how much income you make, and this budget doesn't even add in other expenses that may show up like: oil changes, car registrations, field trips for your kids, replacing things around your home, toiletries, gifts for occasions, vacations, events, clothing, etc.

But make sure to make your budget anyway! It will give you a rough idea of how much you'll be able to put aside later on, and help you to stay on track with your spending.

You may not know the exact numbers, but at least you have a guide and an estimate of how much you should be spending monthly.

Business Monthly Income:

$2,000 (after taxes)

Business Monthly Expenses:

Tax Software $10

Microsoft Word $10

Email Marketing Software $10

Virtual Assistants $120

Stock Photos $10

Recurring Memberships To Courses $100

Advertising $100

Other Business Expenses $200

Total Monthly Business Expenses: $560

Money Left Over From Personal Expenses-Total Monthly Business Expenses=Total Money Left Over To Save

$1,988-560=$1,428

So as you can see from the example business and personal budgets above, you have to tell your money where to go. If you don't have a plan for your money, it will disappear on things you don't need. If you're just spending without tracking and not sticking to your budget, you're creating disorder and overwhelm for yourself.

Tracking and budgeting will help you create freedom for the long term, just keep in mind that **most millionaires are excellent money managers.**

Action Steps:

1. Get out a sheet of paper and create your household budget for this month: put the month and year at the top of the

paper (think carefully, and add in any special events that may cost extra money this month).

2. Create your business budget on the back or on a separate sheet of paper.

3. Do the math (overall income-expenses) to see how much money you have left over at the end of the month to save

Chapter 5: When and How To Reinvest In Your Business

"Never depend on a single income. Make investments to create a second source." ~Warren Buffet

Reinvesting in your business is extremely important, but you also have to make a living and hit savings goals so you'll have even more money to invest in the long term.

Spend Money on Things That Will Expand Your Knowledge and Increase Your Income

Be very particular about investing in your business and yourself, you should only be spending money on things that will help your income to grow or help you grow as a better person. Don't spend your money on **fancy tools that you don't need.** Right now, stick to the basics. Try to stay away from expensive tools that have high monthly subscription costs.

Advertising Is NEVER a Bad Idea

Advertising your business is never a bad idea, just make sure you know what you're doing and track like crazy. If you're going to advertise, make sure you take a course on it so you won't waste a lot of money "testing". Track conversion rates and do what you can to increase them.

All in all, advertising and promoting your business is never a bad idea, and sometimes you have to pay to play.

Using Money from One Business to Start Another

This is another necessary time to reinvest in your business. It's a great idea to have multiple streams of income. Creating new businesses is what we do best, so instead of borrowing money and going debt; use the profits you have to start another business or add to the current one you have.

Just be wary of overwhelm, you don't want to stray from your focus. Your best bet is to hit a certain income goal with your one business or project before moving on to the next.

As you see your money increase, you will be tempted to spend more money on stuff that you don't necessarily need in your business, so before making any purchasing decisions. Think about it for at least a day, and if you still have the same excitement and are willing to be committed, buy it.

Reinvest For Tax Reasons

If you reinvest the profits that you make from your business back into your business such as buying new software, equipment, hiring contractors, etc. You can write off more expenses when tax time comes.

I'm not an accountant, so I can't speak that much on this. But make sure you look for all the tax breaks that you can. Reinvesting is not a bad thing, sometimes it can pay off in the long term. Take time to learn more about taxable income and non-taxable income.

Make Sure To Save

While reinvesting is a great thing to grow your business and pay less taxes, you want to make sure you still put aside some money to save. You don't want ALL your money to be tied up in your business, you want to have some cash for contingencies, fun, salary, and more.

There's not point of working so hard if you can't spend some of the money you've earned on things you enjoy; of course there's a place to draw the line. And becoming smarter with your money will eventually grant you the freedom to spend as much as you want on whatever you like.

You will fill most free when you know you have the money to spend and still have saved in the bank. Manage your money well, and you will have no problem spending some money.

Action Steps:

1. Invest in programs, courses, coaches and books. Things that will increase your skills and knowledge, which in turn will increase your income.

2. Research how to get more tax breaks by reinvesting your money back into your business.

Chapter 6: Debt

"A man in debt is so far a slave." ~Ralph Waldo Emerson

In this chapter, we're going to go into debt, how to avoid it, and how to get rid of it. Most of us are in debt, and the only time debt is a good thing is when it involves the right business, the only business I can think about going into debt over is real-estate.

All other businesses can easily be started by using your own money (at least the ones I'm into building). I'm a digital entrepreneur, so it didn't take much money to get started. I used the money from the day job I was working at to start my businesses.

I understand everyone's story is different, I respect that. Just keep in mind that it is possible to build a profitable business without getting a loan or going into debt.

I only have college debt, because I was fortunate enough to have found entrepreneurship and started reading books about managing your money, so I've always avoided credit cards like the plague. But I will eventually be getting into real-estate and I need to build my credit, plus you get points for traveling, those are the only reasons I'm considering opening a credit card.

How to Decrease Credit Card Debt

Disclaimer: I don't have any credit card debt, so take the advice from this section at your own risk.

Although I don't have credit cards, I've read a lot of financial books on money management and getting out of debt, so I think I may be able to speak on it a little.

One of the takeaways I've got from these books is to pay off the lowest amount of debt first. This will give you confidence to take on the higher amounts later.

Another thing you can do is pay off the credit cards with the highest interest rates first. NO matter what the interest rate is, you'll be paying a lower amount the more you pay it down.

Come up with a plan to pay off your cards. Don't avoid the amounts anymore and write down what you owe. Once you get the big picture, come up with a plan to pay off one of the credit cards while still paying the minimum on the others.

A plan will get you far, but taking action on the plan will get you out of debt. Commit to your plan and follow it. You deserve to live debt free.

College Debt

Yeah, I went to college. I don't talk about it much because it's not that big of a deal. I got my bachelor's degree in Biology from Indiana University of PA. Good times. **I freaking hate biology.** Long story, if you want to learn more about it, email me.

Anyway, not matter how much I hate biology, I still have to pay off the debt I accumulated from the courses I sat in. I went to a state school, so I can't even complain about the amount. It was about $15k when I graduated. I'm about $10k now.

At first I was freaking out about paying it back, but now I just make the monthly payments and think about it as another bill. There's no reason to freak out about it because I know people who get $50k or more into debt after college. I'm grateful my debt is so low.

Also, what's the rush? I'm paying them back. They'll get their money. But I'd rather save money and pay myself first before I rush into paying off school debt.

If you have school debt, and that's the only kind you have. Simply make your monthly payments and don't freak out about it. It's a better debt to have rather than credit card debt. At the time it was an investment in your future plans, and I'm sure you've made connections and had experiences there that you couldn't get anywhere else.

You do want to make your monthly payments though, don't let your loans go into default. Pay your monthly fees. The lenders are willing to work a payment plan out with you. Don't avoid these loans! I've heard horror stories of people getting their wages garnished, when you don't take care of your student loans, you're messing with the government and you don't want to do that!

Action Steps:

1. Crate a plan to lower your credit card debt; pay off the smallest balance first while still paying the minimum for your other cards.

2. If you have college debt, continue paying if off monthly; do not let your loans go into default. Set up a payment plan with your lender.

3. Avoid getting into debt unless it's for a business like real-estate; otherwise try to bootstrap your business by saving.

Chapter 7: Retirement & Investing

"To enjoy a long, comfortable retirement, save more today." ~Suze Orman

The time has come, we're going to go into some of the most important aspects that influence your life greatly, investing and retiring.

I know… you love entrepreneurship so much that you NEVER want to retire, right? Well for those of us who want to create a freedom lifestyle and continue to make income for our families even after we die, we have plans on investing and looking at the long term.

Your investment in yourself and in assets now, will continue to pay you year after year, if you know what you're doing.

Disclaimer: I'm not a professional investor, but I'm working on it by getting stuff set up and putting money aside.

I highly recommend you **begin to read books and studying investing**, so you can see your options and begin to start NOW! That's what I'm doing and it feels pretty good. Don't worry about having enough money, just $100 a month may be able to set you up for life, you just have to know where to invest.

Investments over time is what will aid you in your retirement. You can retire much earlier than you expect if you take short cuts by investing more. But in order to invest, you need to have money to do so. That's why it's so crucial to manage your money.

What's Your Number

What the number that you can live off for the rest of your life? How much money do you need right now so you would never have to work another day in your life?

It's different for all of us. Let's say you make $50,000 a year. And you plan on living another 70 years. ($50,000 a year x 70 years= 3.5 million). So it's obvious you wouldn't be able to retire today, unless you hit it big in some way. And what if you want a fancier lifestyle and you don't want to be stuck only being able to spend $50,000 a year; that's even more investment income you need to have coming in.

So you see why it's important to invest now and know your number, so you can have a goal to work toward. So when your investments start making you $50,000 a year passive income; you'll be set. Keep in mind that **$50,000 a year is only $4,167 a month.** I know you can get your investments to make you that much!

What's Your Plan

Okay you know your number, so what's your plan to get there?

How will you increase the income of your business so you can

invest more money for your retirement and long term growth?

Start thinking of and taking action on strategies that you can use to

increase your income. The more you make, the more you can

invest. The more you invest, the **more freedom you create for**

yourself. Always ask yourself if what you're doing is creating more

freedom for your future.

So figure out a plan. What are you going to invest in? Where are

you going to invest? How will you increase your income in order to

invest more?

Answer these questions. Start thinking like a millionaire investor. **Investors make the big money** at the end of the day, not business owners. But you're well on your way because being a business owner is much better than being an employee.

You have to have money to invest, that's why I keep reiterating that **saving and managing your money** is so important! It sets you up for opportunities to invest and create more freedom.

There are tons of things you can invest in, just come up with a plan and start with one. Then you can diversify once you get the ball rolling and start making more income. There's: businesses, stocks and index funds, retirement accounts, mutual funds, bonds, annuities, etc. Start investing today if you can, allow your money to compound!

IRA

An IRA is an individual retirement account, these are great because they allow you to grow your income tax free. Depending on the type of IRA you go with, you won't be taxed until you withdraw the money. Because of the tax benefits, you're only allowed to invest so much a year. Also, you can't withdraw the money until you 60 years old or older or you'll get penalties.

Because of this age restriction, many entrepreneurs rather take their hard earned money and invest it in businesses. But **for those who like to diversify, an IRA is a decent option.**

There are two types of IRAs. Roth IRA and Traditional IRA. The difference between the two are when you pay our taxes on them. With the traditional IRA (tax deferred) you don't pay taxes on your money until you withdraw it; with the ROTH IRA you pay taxes upfront.

Either way can be risky because no one knows if taxes will be higher or lower in the future. This investment strategy is better than a savings account because you can get capital gains through things like mutual funds, stocks, etc. while the money is in the account. So the growth rate has more potential.

To give yourself more flexibility and to keep from going crazy trying to figure out rather to go with the traditional or ROTH, simply open and invest in both!

Action Steps:

1. Find out your number. How much do you need to retire?
2. Map out a plan to increase your income so you can invest more.
3. Find out where you're going to invest (IRA, real-estate, mutual funds, etc.)

Chapter 8: Increase Your Business Income to Save More

"Overcome your barriers, intend the best, and be patient. You will enjoy more balance, more growth, more income, and more fun."
~Jack Canfield

I saved the best for last. This chapter will be about how you can make more money in order to save more money. When you make more money, you won't feel as restricted to what you can do. Just keep in mind that just because you make more money, doesn't mean you need to increase your lifestyle.

Don't live beyond your means. Be smart and save money, invest money, and create more income. You can worry about increasing your lifestyle once you are making the big bucks and have money management skills.

How To Increase Your Results

In business, we work hard and invest in ourselves to do one thing: to increase our results. The better the results the better the life.

The first thing you want to do to increase your results is to take more action. If you don't have the discipline to do what needs done... and more... then you're always going to stay where you're at. You have to keep growing, learning, and adjusting so you can get more results.

Another thing you can do **test and track.** Make sure you test different things in your business to see how they work. See what goes over well and see if the results are worth continuing with that particular action.

Habits To Ensure Increased Success and Productivity

Your habits are what put you in the exact situation you're in now. Your current circumstances are the result of your habits.

So if you have detrimental habits like: spending every penny you earn, not working on your business, watching 3 hours of T.V. a day, and allowing distractions to come in and take over your schedule— you're most likely having mediocre success.

Success Habits

Start creating habits similar to those that are already successful. You can figure out what habits these are by doing similar things to those who are already successful. There's no need to reinvent the wheel. Just come up with daily success habits that will aid you in getting the results you seek. Here are some to start implementing:

- Working out

- Eating healthy

- Working on income producing activities

- Setting and looking at your goals

- Hanging out with like-minded entrepreneurs

- Connecting with influencers

- Waking up early

- Reading books that will increase your skills

- Planning your weeks

- Listening to audios, video, courses, etc. and taking action on them

- Etc.

While you're still building your business big, you want to make sure you're spending less time on entertainment and more time on personal development and growth.

Morning Routine

Develop a morning routine. How you start your day impacts your entire day. If you start it off right, it'll put you in the right state of mind to take on what you have planned. Do this every single morning, keep in mind that it's best to have a set time you wake up. Here's some examples of what you can incorporate into your morning routine:

- Drink water

- Do a good morning stretch

- Read affirmations

- Look at vision board

- Journal

- Mediate

- Watch motivational video or listen to audio

- Write goals over and review goals

- Read 10 pages of a book

- Work out

Those are just some of the many things you can do to start your day off right. Create your own morning routine and put it into practice. You'll feel amazing each morning before you get your day started.

Night Routine

Create a night routine. Personally, my night routine is not that long. But, it keeps me focused on what I work so hard for every day. You may want to pick a time to go to bed, but you don't have to. But if you want your body to be well rested, it's best to put it on a schedule.

Here is what I do at night:

- Read affirmations

- Look at vision board

- Write goals over and review goals

Your night routine is just as important as your morning routine. You want to make sure you hit the bed with good intentions and excited to conquer tomorrow.

Do What You're Afraid To Do

This is one of the harder things, but it's one of the things that will allow you to grow daily. The more you do what you're afraid to do, you become more fearless and confident.

Start working on those things you've been putting off because you're subconsciously afraid to get started. You know in your mind what will take you to the next level, so whatever your biggest fear is right now; begin taking action on it. I know that it's easier said than done.

Especially for introverts like me, but I still manage to do things that I'm afraid to; and every time I do I see my income grow and my confidence grow.

I'm sure there's a lot you fear, make a list and start with one thing. If you can do one thing today that you're afraid to do, you'll be on your way to massive success.

Find A Mentor

Find a mentor or coach, keep in mind that it's not always free. Sometimes free things aren't very valuable and the great thing about paying is that you'll take it more seriously.

They say you should have a coach in every area of your life, right now just focus on one for your business growth. Our goal here is to increase your income so you can save more money. So once you find a legitimate coach for the business you're in, you'll be able to go to the next level.

The great thing about coaches is they know exactly how to get you to the next level, because they've already been where you are.

A coach may not be cheap. But don't think about how much it's going to cost you, think about how much it's going to make you. If you can't find a coach or can't afford one right now, consider taking a course by the person you want to eventually coach you.

Get results with the course, book, or videos they have, and let them know about it. Become their next success story and then you should be able to get their attention while still having an increased income.

Take A Course

Take a course or read a book that will increase your value and your skills. This is the way I got started seeing money come into my business. Before I was seeking for free information, once I put my money where my mouth is I started to see results.

But it's not enough to just take the course or read the book, you have to put each teaching into action and consistently do so until you see results. And **the results will come, just keep pushing.**

Increase Your Conversion Rates

I'm sure you have something for sale, and if you want to create more income in your business you need to start doing more testing and tracking. See how you can increase the conversion rates by split testing, paying close attention to numbers, and tweaking as you go along.

You should know what your best selling products are, where you traffic is coming from, and who your customers are. Always be mindful of these metrics.

Also, keep good records so you can see how much income you have coming in and going out, start managing your money down to the penny!

Take On Another Project or Scale

Another way to increase your income is to take on another project or business. Depending on your business, you should be able to do this. That's why I like building passive income businesses and online businesses because you can easily leverage them, and don't have to be there to make profits.

If you want to focus on your one business, consider scaling the business you have. Hire more people or contractors to free up your time so you can focus on creating more income.

Bring In Systems or Vas

Bring in systems or Vas to leverage your time and create more income for you. Allowing Virtual Assistants to do your non income producing activities will allow you to get more of the money making tasks done.

Or if you're able to, set up systems that where you don't have to be present to be making money. Things such as email autoresponders, websites, and customer service teams will allow you to focus on what matters most, creating more income.

Look For Tax Breaks

Don't let the IRS rob you of your savings and income. Always be looking at ways that you can get tax breaks or grow your money tax free.

Simple things like re-investing your business income and keeping good records of expenses can help out a lot. Do your research on how to get the most tax breaks out of your business; or hire a CPA that's very knowledgeable about your industry.

Write off everything you can and always be looking for ways to save money on taxes.

Change Your Circle Of Influence

Start getting around like-minded entrepreneurs like yourself. This can be at events, connecting on social media, etc. Once you get around people that are doing big things, you'll begin to raise your standards.

Hang out less with those that don't necessarily have the same success mindset as you, avoid those who are comfortable with being mediocre. Get around influencers that are making the kind of money you want to make and **living the type of lifestyle you want to live.**

By being around successful people, you'll begin to learn more and earn more. I'm going to say it again, sometimes you have to pay to play. It's like a shortcut to getting where you want to go faster. Invest in the people you want to be like.

Network with Like-Minded Entrepreneurs

Always look to connect with like-minded entrepreneurs, this will help to inspire you and you can never have too many connections. When reaching out to people, make sure to come from a place of trying to add value.

Ask what you can do for them or how you can help them get to the next level. Once you've made a ton of friends, you'll see how that comes in handy in the long run. You now have a network of people to refer people to and people that will refer customers to you as well.

You'll always be up on the latest, and you'll know people that can help you out when you're trying something new. It's just always great to connect and meet new people.

Action Steps:

1. Increase your results by working harder and smarter

2. Create success habits

3. Find a mentor

4. Increase Your Skills

5. Change your circle of influence

6. Network with like-minded entrepreneurs daily

Your Feedback Is A Gift

Thank you very much for reading *How To Save Money For Entrepreneurs*, I hope this book inspired you to save a ton of cash and to become a better entrepreneur.

Your feedback is a gift! If you got ANY value out of this book, please pay it forward and leave a review.

Reviews will help other entrepreneurs find the book, and it will also give me feedback on what I've done well or what I can improve on.

About The Author

Greetings! I'm Argena Olivis, author, coach, and serial entrepreneur from Pittsburgh, PA. I make a full time income online, and my goal is to inspire other like-minded entrepreneurs to do the same.

I'm have specialties in different industries such as internet marketing, ecommerce, network marketing, and personal development.

My mission is to help and inspire other entrepreneurs to build the business and lifestyle of their dreams.

To learn more about me, visit my site at http://www.ArgenaOlivis.com/

Check Out My Other Books

Below you'll find some of my other popular books that are popular on Amazon and Kindle as well. Simply click on the links below to check them out. Alternatively, you can visit my author page on Amazon to see other work done by me.

Online Business Mindset: Personal Development and Confidence Building For Internet Marketers

Fulfillment By Amazon For Beginners: Step By Step Instructions On How To Make an Income With FBA

Information Products For Beginners: How To Create and Make Money With Information

Bonus: Download Your Free Kindle Book Creation Course

Learn how to create and market your first kindle book online.

You can use this course to get started making money online.

Plus, when you subscribe you'll receive my best tips and tutorials for online business success.

Learn how I'm making money from the following methods: kindle publishing, affiliate marketing, email marketing, information products, blogging, and more.

Visit www.argenaolivis.com/freekindlecourse2/ for access

www.ingramcontent.com/pod-product-compliance
Lightning Source LLC
Chambersburg PA
CBHW051342170526
45166CB00002B/927